HOUSEPLANTS

D0800054

WILLIAM DAVIDSON

COLLINS

Products mentioned in this book

ICI Antkiller	contains	pirimiphos-methyl
'Keriguard'	contains	dimethoate
'Keriroot'	contains	NAA + captan
'Kerispray'	contains	pirimiphos-methyl

Read the label before you buy; use pesticides safely

Editors Maggie Daykin, Joey Chapter
Designer Chris Walker
Production Controller Craig Chubb
Picture research Moira McIlroy

First published 1990 by
William Collins Sons & Co Ltd
London · Glasgow · Sydney
Auckland · Toronto · Johannesburg

© Marshall Cavendish Limited 1990

British Library Cataloguing in Publication Data

Davidson, William
    Houseplants. — (Collins Aura garden handbooks).
    1. Houseplants
    I. Title
A CIP catalogue record for this book is available from the British Library

ISBN 0-00-412527-4

Typeset by Litho Link Ltd., Welshpool, Powys, Wales
Printed and bound in Hong Kong by Dai Nippon Printing
Company

Front cover: Houseplant group by Marshall Cavendish Library
Back cover: Coleus blumei by Michael Warren

CONTENTS

INTRODUCTION

The term 'houseplant' was first used by Tom Rochford who, at his nursery in Hertfordshire, began propagating and raising a few foliage plants at the end of World War 2. Mr. Tom, as we all knew him, had a great love of plants and a strong feeling that his houseplants had a future – as indeed they had. They grew and prospered to the point where, today, there are few homes that cannot muster at least a small collection of attractive foliage and flowering potted plants.

Since those early days, when we in the nursery used to refer rather disparagingly to Mr. Tom's small collection of cuttings as 'weeds', the scene has changed considerably. A quite incredible number of plants is now sold from an increasingly wide range of outlets.

And while many plants are still locally grown, the vast majority come from around the globe, some as propagating material to be grown on, others as mature plants needing only a brief settling down period before being ready to be put on sale.

Cost effective Surprisingly, as the years have gone by, the cost of plants has not increased all that much – certainly not in proportion to their popularity – and the quality, if anything, has improved.

There are plants to meet almost every taste, from monster ones for the interior decoration of hotels, hospitals and offices, to colourful and difficult kinds to challenge the adventurous home grower, and easy care plants for beginners or those who love to have greenery and flowers in the home but lead busy lives

TOP RIGHT A delightful mixed arrangement of flowering and foliage plants, including pink and white cineraria, cyclamen, primulas and a glossy leaved Bird's Nest Fern.

RIGHT Spectacularly decorative caladium can make an impressive display in their own right, as this mixed group clearly shows.

LEFT *Ficus benjamina* will eventually grow to tree height, if given its head, but can be contained. Its slender pointed leaves and graceful weeping habit make it a very popular choice as a floor-standing plant for any room.

that leave little time for plant care.

Interior designers find them useful and attractive accessories in many different schemes, while young people furnishing their first home on a tight budget quickly discover that large, sculptural plants fill a spare corner nicely until the time comes when just the right piece of furniture can be afforded.

Wide choice There really is a good choice of plants to suit any location. There are busy climbers and trailers, handsome palms, grassy-leaved plants, frondy ferns, lobed plants, spear-leaved ones, indoor bulbs, cacti and succulents and even miniature trees.

Every conceivable shape, size, habit and colouring is available to delight, inspire or challenge you. And once you start propagating your own, you will have embarked on a hobby that could last a lifetime, and will certainly give you many hours of pleasure.

My own working life has been a story of plants: growing, displaying, talking and writing about them, and always it has been my view that plants are there to be enjoyed, not to be fretted over all the time. In fact, it may seem an odd comment, but plants rarely grow well for miserable people – so give them a smile!

BUYING HOUSEPLANTS

There are all sorts of reasons why one may have success or failure with indoor plants and, surprisingly, owners are almost too willing to blame themselves when a plant does not flourish. They rarely look deeper into the problem than that they might have overwatered or overfed it. But if you know what to look for when you are buying houseplants, you can avoid most of these disappointments.

Whether buying plants to be displayed in splendid isolation or, as here, effectively grouped to offset one another, healthy plants will give lasting value. The draceana, calathea and dieffenbachia shown are clearly in peak condition.

There was a time when plants were sold mainly by retailers who knew what was needed in the way of care and attention, and where they could buy for resale the best plants available. But nowadays, all sorts of people add potted plants to the various other sundry items that they sell. If you purchase plants from this kind of retailer soon after they arrive at his or her premises then there could well be no difficulty, but if you were to buy the same plants after a week out on the pavement with little or no attention, they could be virtually dead before you even get them home and in position.

Quality counts So, the first lesson in plant care is to buy good quality plants from a reliable retailer, plants that will have an infinitely better chance of surviving once introduced to indoor conditions that may be vastly different from the warm and humid greenhouse in which they were raised. The plants should look fresh and lively and not be hanging their heads as if they were ashamed to be on display.

Some retail premises are inadequately heated during the hours of darkness, or at other times when customers are not about, and this lowering of temperature can be damaging to almost all the more delicate plants. One of the plants that is particularly sensitive to low temperatures is the dieffenbachia, greatly prized for its ornamental foliage. If you see this one with its leaves drooping instead of standing out firmly from the stem then you will know that night temperatures have been too low and that your plant purchase ought to be made from an outlet that is more sensitive to plants' needs.

Knowledgeable staff The sales staff ought to know their plants and be able to answer any questions that you have. If these skills are questionable then their ability to care for potted plants may be equally suspect. They should be able to tell you which ones are most likely to do well in your home, once you have briefly described the location you have planned for your purchase. And it is wise to listen to such advice and buy the sort of plant that is likely to do well rather than something too delicate or too exotic for your conditions or your skills to be able to cope with.

If you are a beginner with indoor plants, make this clear to the assistant so that reasonably easy plants may be recommended. Practise your skills and learn with these plants and when they are doing well there will be ample time to become more adventurous and test your expertise.

Poinsettia (Euphorbia pulcherrima) is a spectacular plant to give or receive as a gift, particularly popular at Christmas. When buying, however, beware of a plant that has few lower leaves. They may have been removed to disguise the fact that the plant is suffering from botrytis.

When greeted by a display as colourful and beguiling as this one, it is all too easy to pick up the nearest pot that appeals to you. But better to take your time and inspect several carefully before making your choice. Check both foliage and flowers for signs of problems.

If there is no assistant from whom specialist advice can be acquired then it would be wise to take with you this book giving clear advice on what is easy and what is difficult among the many plants that will be available. Some, in fact most these days, will have care tags in the plant pot that may prove useful when you are making your decision. Whether or not they indicate how easy it is to grow the plant, such labels should always tell you the most appropriate temperature, siting and watering needs. You will probably want to remove the tag but do keep it close by, at least initially. It will serve as a handy reminder.

Specialist nurseries and shops apart, many High Street stores offer better plants than you will find anywhere. This is because they set strict guidelines for the grower to follow, with the result that their plants are received in prime condition. Their premises are also warm and adequately lighted so that your purchase should give you maximum pleasure when you get it home – if you afford it reasonable care.

What to look for First look at the general cleanliness of the shop or store, and then inspect the plants for the freshness of their foliage, and in the case of flowering kinds check that they have not become overblown as a result of being too long in transit, or on display. Plants with yellowing leaves ought to be avoided, also those that have clearly lost leaves at the base. Also, look closely among the leaf and flower stalks of plants to ensure that there are no fungal problems such as botrytis that will quickly destroy the plant once you have taken it indoors. Look, too, for white powdery spots on plant leaves – these indicate the presence of mildew and generally poor growing conditions at some stage in the plant's development. Many begonias are particularly susceptible to mildew, so careful inspection is needed when making one's choice.

Look, also, for the presence of pests, as there is no reason for taking any of these home, perhaps to contaminate other plants in one's collection. White fly can be extremely difficult to get rid of once they have set up home, but they are easily detected on the undersides of leaves when the plant is held up for inspection. Or the plant can be gently brushed with a hand for any white fly that may be present to be seen flying away from the plant. Poinsettias, widely available around Christmas time, are especially susceptible to white fly.

Look for aphids on all sorts of plants, and pay special attention to the softer growth areas of the plant. In the case of hibiscus plants, aphids generally congregate around the unopened flower buds. These pests are not difficult to control, but why purchase them if it can be avoided? Look for the presence of mealy bug (a waxy cottonwool-like substance in the more inaccessible areas of plants is their trade mark) among the foliage of larger ferns, stephanotis and around the spines of cacti. Pale brown discoloration of leaves that are normally bright green may well indicate that red spider mites are in attendance – avoid such plants as these mites can become very troublesome once established.

The good news is that these pests are seen only at inferior establishments. In general, the problem of pests is very strictly controlled at all commercial nurseries, so you should not have many problems when plants are being bought.

Lastly, when you have made your purchase be sure that in cold weather it is properly wrapped for the journey home. And never put plants in the cold boot of the car – better by far for them to be with you in the warmer area. Exposure to cold conditions for even a brief period can prove to be a considerable setback to a tender plant from the tropics.

ABOVE When buying a mixed grouping in a bowl, always check whether there is good drainage.

LEFT If your new plant is destined to join a prized collection such as this one, it is well worth the time it takes to check that the plant is healthy.

PROPAGATION

When you see the vast numbers of houseplants that are on sale you may well wonder where all the propagating material comes from to make the plants in the first place. Much of the more exotic material comes from tropical regions of the world; cuttings are flown to commercial growers in Europe to be prepared and inserted in vast beds of propagating compost and later potted and grown on.

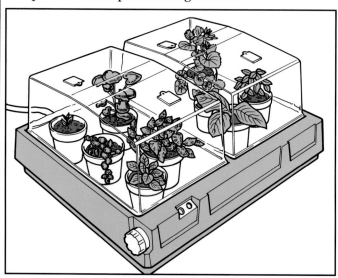

If you are propagating plants only on a small scale, then it is perfectly possible to manage without a propagator. A polythene bag held clear of the cuttings by three or four small canes will suffice. But for propagating on a larger scale you will find a propagator is an invaluable friend.

Of course, that is only part of the story. Some nurseries specialise in the rooting and supply of materials ready for potting. And mature plants are also flown in from abroad to enjoy a short period in a grower's greenhouse before being sold.

But this is a far cry from someone with a few plants on the windowsill who wishes to try propagating them. And while you can very easily buy more plants, there is something special about sharpening the knife, removing the cutting and inserting it in the pot of compost – and then watching its progress. And there is no reason why you should not emulate the professional grower's efforts to some extent, even if you have only a windowsill on which to do this.

The first thing you will need is clean compost – a mix of peat and sand not being a bad start. Then perhaps a small heated propagator – if you can employ a small propagator with bottom heat the cuttings are less likely to damp off and will develop roots much more readily. You will also need clean, preferably small pots, a sharp knife and good quality plants from which to take cuttings; inferior cuttings would simply mean inferior results. So remove the best material, be it from a tradescantia, ivy, begonia or whatever. Start with the easily propagated plants, as they will be your stepping stones to trying your increasing skills on some of the more testing subjects later on.

Plantlets The very easiest plants to propagate are those that form small plantlets while still attached to the parent. Chief among these must be the Spider Plant that, as the parent plant ages, produces long, stem-like growths, on the ends of which develop young plants that are perfect replicas of the parent. Leave these 'babies' attached to the stalk, but peg them down in pots of compost until they produce roots of their own, when they can be snipped from the parent to become individual plants already potted.

Another plant of this type is *Saxifraga sarmentosa*, Mother of Thousands, which has masses of dangling babies on thin strands of growth.

Tolmiea menziesii, the Pick-a-back Plant, develops miniature plants on the backs of parent leaves and these can be removed and firmly planted in pots of compost, where they will very soon produce roots of their own. In similar fashion, *Episcia dianthiflora* produces its growth in neat rosettes of leaves and these can be taken off when of an appropriate size to start life on their own.

If you have reasonably warm conditions Bromeliads will also be similarly easy to increase. Having flowered, the main plant of the bromeliad will die, but this does not mean that it is time to go out and buy a replacement. As the flower dies and the main rosette of the bromeliad begins to lose its appearance small plants develop at the base of the parent stem. The old rosette can be cut away when no longer attractive and the new plantlets allowed to develop, as a cluster, to a reasonable size before removing them with a sharp knife and potting them individually.

LEFT To increase a *Tolmiea menziesii*, remove the parent leaf and pot it up with its stem buried and plantlet resting on the soil's surface. Keep moist.

ABOVE AND BELOW This *Chlorophytum comosum* can have its young plantlets potted alongside the parent and detached when rooted. They also root in water.

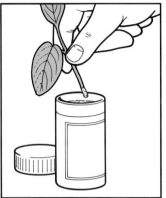

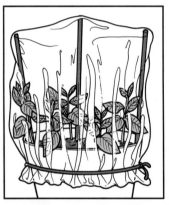

FAR LEFT For stem cuttings, cut a piece of healthy young stem, about 10cm (4in) long.

LEFT Remove the lower leaves then dip the base of cutting in rooting powder. Shake off excess.

BELOW FAR LEFT Fill a plastic pot with compost formulated for cuttings. Make a hole with a dibber and insert the treated cutting. Firm well in. Repeat round edge of pot with other cuttings.

LEFT Improvise a propagator by inserting canes into the soil as supports and cover with a polythene bag, secured to the rim by rubber bands.

Stem cuttings Ivies are among my favourite plants and these are best propagated in late spring or summer. Take fresh strands of growth and cut them up into sections of stem with two leaves attached. Then treat the part of the stem to be inserted in the compost by first dipping it into rooting powder such as 'Keriroot' and insert five to seven cuttings in each 7.5cm (3in) pot. By putting in a nice lot of cuttings you will find that attractive plants are available at a much earlier stage. Tradescantias can be propagated in much the same way – lots of cuttings to each pot – best taken from the top 7.5cm (3in) or so of the plant.

Leaf cuttings If you are in the mood for a challenge you could experiment with cuttings of *Begonia rex*, but you will need a heated propagator for this. Take a firm, mature leaf from the plant and cut the leaf stalk back to about 2.5cm (1in) from the leaf. Turn the leaf face down on a flat surface and with the knife make several cuts through the veins of the leaf; then place the leaf, pretty side uppermost, on a bed of moist peat in a seed tray or large pan. Use a few hairpins or bent wire to pierce the leaf and hold it in position. If the interior of the propagator is kept warm and moist, you should eventually find little plantlets growing.

Division Another relatively easy method of increasing plants is by division. Two of the best subjects for this method of propagation are the spathiphyllum and the dear old aspidistra – though the latter is now a very much less popular plant. However, if you have a very old aspidistra, do water it before you remove it from its container. You will find that it has developed a very solid centre around which the leaves are emerging. Traditionally, you should tease the roots apart, but these older plants usually need a saw to cut the clump into manageable sections. Having got the sections you then simply pot them up into pots of appropriate size, to be grown on as individual plants.

A much more popular and very attractive plant, the spathiphyllum is also propagated by first watering the plant then removing it from its pot so that a strong, sharp knife can be employed to divide the clump into sections which are then potted separately. This form of propagation is one that virtually everyone ought to be successful with.

Seeds For large numbers of plants, increasing your stock would involve sowing seed; many flowering and foliage plants can be done in this way. Again, you will need clean, warm and agreeable conditions in order to be successful with seed raising, and you should follow the directions on the seed packet.

FAR RIGHT An ideal subject for propagating by means of leaf cuttings is the long-leaved sansevieria.

RIGHT Select a strong, healthy leaf and sever it from the plant. Place the leaf on a flat surface and cut into sections, as shown (about four pieces from a leaf).

RIGHT Insert the lower half of each section into potting compost and new plantlets will form. Do not overwater or the cuttings will soon rot.

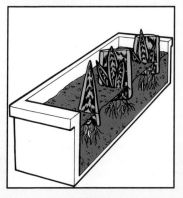

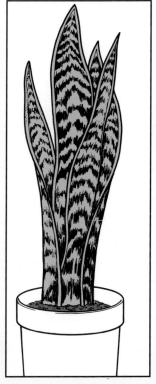

AFTERCARE

The purchase of healthy plants at the outset has already been mentioned, and it cannot be too heavily stressed that getting them off to a good start will make all the difference in the world to the general success of houseplant growing.

Some people say that they have black fingers and can never grow any sort of plant successfully indoors, but one often wonders if the conditions in that person's home are not more to blame. On the subject of fingers, you may well ask, 'Do people really have "green fingers"?' My answer would be, 'Yes, there are fortunate people who have a natural ability when it comes to caring for plants, be they indoor or out.' You may find that you are gifted in this way. But let us take the newly acquired plant, fresh from its place with its friends in the nice warm and humid greenhouse – what is it most likely to want on arrival in the strange new surroundings that are, in fact, your home?

Temperature Reasonable warmth is essential to almost all indoor plants, with 15°C (60°F) being suggested as a minimum to encourage your new plant to settle and make fresh growth. While cooler growing plants such as chlorophytum will tolerate higher temperatures it will be difficult for such plants as calatheas to survive at temperatures below 15°C (60°F).

When positioning plants, it is important to keep them away from radiators, in particular to avoid placing them above radiators in the ascending stream of hot air. If electrical fan heaters are in use, plants must never stand in the stream of hot air. Rooms that are excessively hot will also be detrimental to plants as the air dries out and plants lose much of their vitality. Also, in high temperatures and dry atmosphere there will be a tendency for the minute but damaging red spider mites to be more active. If an even temperature can be maintained it will be much better for plants than temperatures that fluctuate.

Light Almost regardless of the window area in the room, the levels of light will be very much lower than that which the plant enjoyed in its greenhouse location. And if a light meter is used it will be found that

16

with every step one takes back from the window there is a marked reduction in the available light. There are foliage plants that will tolerate lower light levels, particularly those with entirely green foliage such as philodendrons, and many ferns, but even those will fare better in good light provided that it is not too bright and sunny.

Flowering plants must have good light if they are to develop flower buds and eventually flowers, with direct sunlight not being too much of a problem provided it is not fiercely hot. Very strong sunlight is magnified by the glass of the window pane with the distinctly possible result that foliage will be scorched and flowers will fade and go over more quickly than they ought. Bear this in mind when siting your plants.

One of the most frequent questions asked by growers of indoor plants relates to the fact that they are unable to get African Violets to flower for a second time indoors. And the answer has as much to do with light levels as anything. To encourage flowering of these plants they should have a light window location during the day and additional, artificial light in the evening. In fact, placing a light over one's plants in the evening, be they flowering or foliage, will considerably enhance their appearance and encourage growth. Lights placed too near to plants can be damaging, however, so care is needed; at the first sign of a bad reaction, move the light source a little further away or, probably more convenient, move the plants until you get it right.

LEFT The adiantums are shade-loving ferns – but that does not mean that they do not need light. They should be kept out of direct sunlight but when set a little distance from a window, as here, the delicate, finely cut fronds of *Adiantum raddianum* are seen to perfection.

RIGHT Flowering plants in particular need good light if they are to give of their best. This grouping of primulas, variegated ivy and ferns is placed near an artificial light source in the evenings.

High temperatures – whether due to central heating or a heatwave – will take their toll of houseplants, unless you make due provision. One excellent way to ensure that plants retain sufficient moisture is to place them on a gravel-filled tray. Simply keep the gravel moist and the plants will flourish.

Humidity Mention has been made of high temperatures drying out the atmosphere and causing stress to many plants, so something should be done to offset this difficulty if your home is a bit of a hot house. The simplest and least costly way of doing this is to provide a watertight dish or tray for plants to stand on. Also, before placing the plants, the tray should be filled with a moisture-retaining material. There are any number to choose from — capillary matting, wet gravel, wet sand, peat, even layers of newspaper. For this sort of situation, plastic pots are better than those made from clay because the plastic pot has a very thin base and once the pot is placed on the wet base material the compost in the pot will make immediate contact and beneficial capillary action can then take place.

The plant-filled tray can become an important feature in the room, particularly if a light is placed over it. Plants also grow very much better in the company of other plants and with a reasonably large tray one can get a lot of pleasure from arranging the plants in a way that gives them most appeal.

For the individual plant, a pot saucer can be filled with grit, or some other moisture-retaining material for the plant to stand on and enjoy a reasonable amount of humidity around its leaves. It is sometimes advocated that the growing pot should be placed in a larger pot and the space between them filled with moist peat, but this can lead to the plant becoming much too wet. It is important that the compost around the roots of the plant should be able to drain freely and relatively quickly every time that water has been poured on to its surface.

Watering When watering plants, it is important that there should be no sluggishness in the drainage of water through the compost. If, when water is applied to the surface of the compost, there is a tendency for it to remain there rather than drain through it is an indication that the drainage holes in the bottom of the pot are restricted. Invert the pot with one hand over the soil surface and tap the side of the pot on a table edge to loosen the plant so that the rootball can be removed for a thorough inspection.

Plants deteriorate rapidly in badly drained soil, and the most common cause of this sort of blockage is worm casts filling the drainage holes in the pot so that water cannot escape. Worms are easily detected in the compost and can be removed when seen.

Capillary matting is the ideal longer term method of keeping plants moist when, for instance, you go away on holiday.

Drainage may also be restricted if the soil surface becomes compacted, and the way to deal with this is to use a pencil to break up the top layer of soil and remove it, then replace it with fresh compost. The latter is, in fact, a worthwhile annual exercise; blocked drainage or not, this will help aerate the soil, provide a little fresh nourishment for surface roots and greatly improve the general appearance of the plant.

Golden rules with water are that it should be given more freely in spring and summer and very sparingly in winter when plants are less active. With a few exceptions, plants also do better if the soil is allowed to dry out reasonably between each watering rather than be wet all the time. When plants are potted, a little depth should be left between the rim of the pot and the top of the compost so that when plants are watered a reasonable amount is briefly held in this surface area before draining through. If plants become slightly dry, water will initially drain through more slowly, so it is wise to pour just a little on to the surface of the soil and wait until it drains through before giving further water.

There are very few plants that like to be wet all the time, but one of those is *Azalea indica* and the way to water this is to hold the rim of the pot in your fingers with your thumbs on the soil, and then submerge the pot in a bucket of water until all the bubbles have escaped.

Very cold water can be a bother to some plants, so always have a can of water that has been standing in a warm room for about 24 hours so that it has lost its chill feeling before plants are watered. Make a practice of watering the plants then refilling the can straight away, in readiness for the next round of watering.

Commercial growers never place their plants in water dishes, yet the advice is freely offered that plants should be placed in saucers of water so that they may draw up moisture from the bottom, thus avoiding getting water on flowers or foliage. African Violets and cyclamen in particular seem to come in for a lot of such advice. But by using a narrow-spouted watering can and carefully pouring water on to the soil there should be no need for splashing it all round the foliage and flowers as you do so.

My fear, when suggesting watering from the bottom, is that plants can become very much too wet at their roots — waterlogged so that all air is excluded from around them. The result of this is that roots rot and die. Modern composts are composed almost entirely of peat, which acts like a sponge and sucks up far more water than the plant is ever likely to need, unless it happens to be the water-demanding azalea.

Whatever the method of watering, it is of the utmost importance that the complete rootball is wetted – a dribble of water wetting the top inch or so of soil in the pot will be of little or no benefit to the plant. Often enough one sees plants that are obviously under stress, yet the surface of the soil in the pot seems to indicate that the compost is wet. However, simply by lifting the pot and feeling the weight you can tell it is dry at the roots. The bulk of the root system will be in the lower third of the pot and if water is not getting to this area then the plant will suffer. Be sure when you water that surplus liquid is seen to drain through the holes in the bottom of the pot and into the saucer or tray.

Another way of providing moisture for indoor plants is to use a hand spray to mist over their foliage and around the containers in which the plants are growing – this will certainly lift humidity levels in very warm rooms. But, in my experience,

Regular spraying of most houseplants is neither necessary nor advisable. But when you are dealing with one that has many small variegated leaves, as in the case of this ivy, an occasional spray provides a quick springclean. Stand the plant on an upturned bowl or pot in a sink or washbasin and spray lightly.

20

this is not an essential practice and can lead to the leaves of plants becoming very dusty through dust adhering to the damp leaves. If spraying over *is* considered necessary it should be done with water at room temperature.

Where plants, such as *Monstera deliciosa*, the Cheese Plant, have moss-covered supports it is essential to the well-being of the plant that the moss is kept moist all the time. These supports encourage the development of the aerial roots of the plant, and consequently the better development of the plant.

You may also come across plants that are growing in containers with no drainage holes in their base – most often in decorative gift arrangements where there are several plants growing in the same bowl or dish. With such containers it is important to ensure that watering is not overdone as surplus water cannot drain away and the roots quickly become waterlogged. The same applies to plants that are grouped in bottle gardens and the currently fashionable terrariums.

Feeding As with watering, the plant's need for food is greater during the spring and summer than it is in autumn and winter. It is generally the best practice to say no more feeding from about the beginning of autumn through to spring, when new growth becomes evident.

Newly acquired plants should be fed from the time they are taken indoors during the growing season, as all of them will have been fed at the nursery where they were grown for several weeks or months prior to being dispatched. There are all sorts of fertilisers on the market for indoor plants, in liquid form, powder form, as tablets to be pushed into the soil or as a foliar feed that is sprayed

on to the foliage. They vary considerably in price, and in performance, so it is a question of deciding what is best for your plants and being sure to follow the directions provided to get the best results. For feeding houseplants, it is best to use a fertilizer developed specifically for them, such as 'Kerigrow' liquid or 'Keriguard' slow release tablets.

Display of indoor plants Dotting plants all around the room is one way of displaying them, but they will look much better if they become an important feature in the room, arranged together on a table or in a tray. At floor level, larger plants grouped together can offer considerable appeal and they seem to flourish in such companionable settings.

A moss-covered support is essential when growing a large plant such as *Monstera deliciosa*. Without such support the aerial roots cannot develop properly and the plant will fail to achieve its quite spectacular full potential.

21

SOILS AND POTTING

Lots of well-meaning advice flies around in connection with potting on plants, and it is not unusual for novice houseplant growers to find this task the most daunting of all. Yet taking the plant from one pot and settling it into another is actually very simple.

A sure sign that your plant needs repotting is when the roots are beginning to crowd the pot, as in the case of this saintpaulia. (You might also want to take this opportunity of dividing the plant to make two.) If simply potting on, follow the steps that are outlined below right.

The advice will often be quite categorical regarding when particular plants should be potted on, but this is a complete nonsense. All plants differ just as humans do, and most growing conditions differ, too, so you cannot say with certainty how often any one should be potted. The best guide is to water the compost and remove the plant from its pot to see just how much root development there is. If there is a lot of root, consider potting the plant on. If there is not, put it back and leave the potting on until a later stage.

Newly purchased plants might well need repotting, and this is particularly so in respect of ferns. If the plant appears too large for the pot in which it is growing, then inspect the roots and repot straight away if they are very crowded.

The best time for potting is early summer when growth is most active,

and the best pot for the purpose is one that will offer about 2.5cm (1in) of space between the new pot and the rootball of the plant, with slightly more space than that at the bottom of the pot.

Following repotting, give the compost a good watering and then leave the plant for 10-14 days before giving it any further water. Plants prefer to be a little on the dry side following potting so that roots develop as they forage for moisture.

The potting compost used for repotting the plant is vital to its future well-being, so choose and prepare it with care. At one time, the John Innes formula potting mixtures were all the rage for potted plants, but the formula of 7 parts loam, 3 peat, 2 sand was inclined to be too heavy for the majority of indoor plants. However, by reversing the amounts of loam and peat: 7 peat and 3 loam, a very acceptable compost can be made. Commercially, there are now three John Innes Formulas: the one for seedlings, which is No 1; No 2 is for the next stage of potting and No 3 for the final potting of plants. A recognized brand of houseplant compost such as 'Kericompost' is made to a precise formula to suit most houseplants.

Soilless composts The majority of composts offered today for the potting of indoor plants is what is termed 'soilless', meaning that they are of peat with appropriate fertilisers added. These mixes tend to be very variable, even from the same manufacturer and often from bag to bag displayed on the same shelf at the retailers.

One of the major problems is that the compost is very often excessively wet and not in any way suitable for potting plants as it stands. You can get over the wet problem to some extent by emptying the compost on to a plastic sack in the garden and spreading it very thinly so that the sun dries it out, or you can add by volume about one third of perlite – available from garden centres. When spreading the compost on the sack, also inspect it for vine weevil grubs which are white in colour with a pinkish head colouring. If you find these, return everything to the retailer as these weevils are very difficult to eradicate.

Finally, never be tempted to put plants into excessively large pots indoors. Once they are in containers of 17.5cm (7in) diameter they can be sustained with feeding and rarely require further potting.

LEFT Select a pot 5cm (2in) wider and deeper than the old one. Put fresh compost in the base (no crocks are needed if using a plastic pot). Place the old empty pot on this base and fill in the space between them with compost.

BELOW LEFT Remove the old pot, leaving its impression.

BELOW Fit the plant into the cavity left and ensure that old and new compost are in contact all round. Water the compost and allow to drain.

PLANT PROBLEMS

Where pests come from, and how they find their way into the living room, is a problem that perplexes many houseplant growers. The answer is that many of those pests come with introduced plants, either bought or, dare I say it, donated by a friend – the latter being the most likely source albeit unwittingly. So bear this in mind and inspect all plants for problems before they are included with the rest of your collection.

Compared to pests, diseases are not such a worrying problem as far as houseplants are concerned. Nevertheless, any plants with blemished foliage or signs of rotting should be passed over in favour of unmarked plants.

Pests are at their most active during the spring and summer months when plants are developing the soft new growth that such marauders feed upon. At these times be most particular about exercising some control. Prevention is clearly the best practice as it can be almost impossible to eradicate pests such as red spider mites and white fly once they become firmly established.

There are many insecticides on the market for controlling these pests, available as sprays, dusts,

To keep your houseplants healthy, it is important to hold at bay any invasion by the small pests detailed here.

slow release tablets and so on. Sprays such as 'Kerispray' are most effective for eradicating leaf pests such as aphids and white fly.

To prevent pest attack, tablets such as 'Keriguard' slowly release insecticide which is taken up by the plant roots and moves to the leaves, giving protection from pests for up to two months.

To control pests in the compost use an insecticide dust such as 'Sybol' Dust, which can be incorporated into the compost when repotting or planting. The following are the pests that one is most likely to come across when caring for indoor plants:

Aphids on cineraria bud.

Both live mainly on any rotting matter in the compost and do little harm, but if they become a worry they can be eradicated by applying a spray of 'Kerispray' to the compost surface and preventing reinvasion by incorporating a small quantity of ICI Antkiller Dust into the surface of the compost.

Mealy bug These resemble wood-lice, and have a powdery coating in their adult form, but their presence is more easily detected by noting the peculiar waxy cottonwool-like coating that mealy bugs wrap around their young. This waxy material offers splendid protection for the babies within as it is almost impossible to penetrate with a spray-on

Mealy bugs on a fern.

Aphids More commonly referred to as greenfly, these may also be black, grey or orange, but they all come under the banner of aphids. These sap-sucking insects favour the soft growing areas of plants, particularly ivies, and the flowers of many house-plants. They are not difficult to control with spray-on type insecticides, such as 'Kerispray'. Apply a light, even cover to the plant but do avoid direct and heavy treatment with aerosol products.

One difficulty is that sprayed insecticides tend to disperse over a wide area. One tip is to take the plant out of doors – particularly if you are using a product that smells. Or ventilate the room well during and after the treatment until satisfied that the smell has dispersed.

Fungus gnats These are black and jump around on the surface of the compost in the pot. There are also symphalids or spring tails that are white and perform in the same way.

25

insecticide. It is best to apply a systemic insecticide such as 'Kerispray', which enters the plant sap and is taken up by the pest when it is feeding. Repeat the treatment at regular intervals until the plant is free of the pest.

Alternatively, wipe the mealy bugs off with a moistened cotton wool bud making sure that all of the pests are removed. These pests get into twining branches and other inaccessible areas of plants – among cacti spines they are very difficult to get at.

Red spider mite Possibly the most debilitating pest of all, in that it sucks the life out of plants so they shrivel up and die. Not easy to detect with the naked eye, they attack soft tissue to begin with. Signs of their presence are pale brown discoloration of foliage that should be green; in severe attacks they form webs on the undersides of leaves and from leaf stalk to the main stem of the plant. At this stage of development the bin is the only place for the plant

attacked and a thorough inspection and treatment of all plants that were adjacent is essential. There are numerous insecticides offered for their control, such as 'Kerispray' but it is important to treat plants thoroughly and often until there is no sign of pest activity.

Scale insects These are found mainly on the stems and undersides of leaves, and are especially fond of citrus plants, *Ficus benjamina* and bay trees. A black sooty deposit on leaves is their trade mark. Plants should be periodically inspected on the undersides of leaves, mainly along the centre vein. Scale insects are almost black when adult and flesh coloured when young.

To control these pests use the systemic insecticide treatment that is recommended for mealy bug. Or rub off those that are accessible with a cotton wool bud.

Vine weevils The greyish-black female is on the wing during spring

Red spider mites on palm.

Scale insects and their damage.

Vine weevils on cyclamen corm.

and eats around various leaves in the home and garden, but it is her offspring, whitish coloured grubs with orange heads, that cause the worst damage. These attack plants' roots and it is usually not until the plant collapses and dies that there is any indication of their presence. Eradication of this pest is very difficult; the best advice is to protect plants, particularly those in con-

tainers. When potting up or repotting mix a small quantity of ICI Antkiller Dust in with the compost and then apply the same dust to the surface of the compost at regular intervals to prevent the recurrence of any further invasion of this kind. Containers that are already infested can be drenched with 'Sybol' solution and then treated with the dust.

White fly To avoid purchasing plants with these flies on the undersides of leaves is the first precaution. Even so, my houseplants almost inevitably get white fly in the spring, but I simply invert the leaves and rub out the pests before they have a chance to multiply. Where larger numbers have built up, you can spray the plants four times at four-day intervals with 'Kerispray', more often in warm weather, and control them that way.

White flies, much enlarged.

SIXTY OF THE BEST

Some of the plants in this special selection are old favourites, some are new ones. A few have had their heyday but still merit our attention. Others offer a challenge to more experienced growers keen to expand their range and skills. All are plants that will greatly enhance interiors with their foliage, or their flowers, or even with both.

Adiantum

There are numerous cultivars of the popular Maidenhair Fern, all having delicate, pale green foliage that is the perfect foil for almost any grouping of assorted plants. These plants abhor bright sunlight, so must have shaded and moist conditions in order to succeed. If purchased plants seem overlarge for the pots they are growing in consider immediate potting on. In early autumn old fronds can be removed to encourage the development of fresh growth.

Aechmea rhodocyiana

As the common name of Urn Plant suggests, the broad and upright, silver-grey leaves of this Bromeliad plant form into an urn shape that is perfectly watertight. Incidentally, this must be kept topped up with water. After a number of years a spectacular pink bract with bright blue flowers emerges from the water reservoir in the centre of the plant and lasts for several months before it shrivels and dies. At this stage the plant develops up to five small plants at the base of the parent rosette and when large enough these can be potted separately. These are easy-care plants.

Adiantum (Maidenhair Fern)

Aechmea rhodocyiana with its spectacular pink bract

30

Aichrysum domesticum
'Variegatum'

This is a succulent with white and green foliage that forms into a neat bush and is very easy to grow if given a light windowsill location. Generally scarce so you have to hunt around a bit to find a supplier. Or on finding a friend has such a plant ask whether you could have a few cuttings; they root very easily.

Aglaonema

Several cultivars are available, the best being *A. roebelinii* 'Silver Queen', which develops rosettes of grey-green foliage. One of the very best plants for poorly-lit locations and much used for underplanting in office interior planting schemes. Keep warm, shaded and moist for best results. (Too much sun would scorch the leaves and make them curl.) Stem cuttings can be propagated easily at any time of the year.

Anthurium scherzerianum

Ananas comosus
'Aureovariegatus'

The variegated pineapple plant has attractive cream and green rosettes of leaves, but vicious spines along their entire margins – careful handling is essential. Easy-care, undemanding plants that may well fruit when grown in a pot. As fruits develop the entire plant becomes suffused with attractive bright pink colouring that few other plants can match. Keep in a good light and avoid very wet conditions but do not let it dry out.

Anthurium

There are several of these colourful plants, but the only one compact enough to be suitable for indoor use is *A. scherzerianum*, Flamingo Flower, which develops a deep pink spathe flower early in the year. Plants must have warm, shaded and moist conditions, but they can be surprisingly tough provided that the temperature is maintained at not less than 15°C (60°F).

Aglaonema roebelinii 'Silver Queen'

Aralia sieboldii

Also listed as *Fatsia japonica*, the green form is the more common, but there is also a fine variegated cultivar – which is a little more difficult to manage. The large, bright green, palmate leaves are excellent if given sufficient space in which to develop, and plants can be hardened off to survive very well out of doors. Red spider mites can be a problem; otherwise this is an easy-care plant and a very handsome one.

Asparagus densiflorus 'Sprengeri'

Bright green needle-like leaves are attached to wiry stems that, in time, attain considerable length – with nasty barbs that must be avoided. Very easy-care plants that are excellent for hanging pots placed where the barbs can do no harm, but check for potting on annually.

Azalea indica

Asparagus densiflorus 'Sprengeri'

Azalea indica

Perhaps the best of all the flowering pot plants, these come in many colours and are evergreen. Cool, moist and lightly shaded conditions suit them best. Water is essential, so hold the pot submerged in a bucket once or twice weekly until all the air bubbles have escaped – dribbles of water on the soil surface will have no use whatever, so be generous. Remove dead flowers and put plants in a shaded spot in the garden for the summer (then bring inside again to avoid frosts). Consider potting them on in acidic or ericaceous compost when they are put out of doors.

Begonia rex

Begonia rex
Grown entirely for their colourful foliage, these will need good light indoors, with reasonable warmth and moist surroundings. The attractive leaves are easily bruised and damaged so handle with care.

Begonia hiernalis Rieger
Many hybrids in lovely colours are now available. The flowers last for many weeks during spring and summer, but can be disappointing at other times. Cool, light and airy conditions are best for prolonging flower life.

Begonia lucerne
This is but one of the many fine cane-type begonias. Leaves are greenish brown on the upper surface and red on the reverse and attached to stems that will attain a height of 1.8m (6ft) or more. Pendulous reddish-pink flowers are an added bonus and are present for a long period from spring onwards. Cuttings root very easily. Warm, light and moist conditions will suit them fine. Excellent for conservatories.

Beloperone guttata
The Shrimp Plant almost invariably looks rather bedraggled when seen in the average home, usually because it is starved of nourishment. These very pleasing plants develop a surprising amount of root and if potting on is not attended to they quickly lose their colour, shed leaves and begin to look very sad – so don't neglect the potting and the feeding.

Billbergia
The two of these Bromeliads that you may come across are B. *nutans* and B. × *windii*, both of which are among the toughest plants ever created, yet they are not popular with the commercial producers.

Billbergia nutans

Seems odd, because they are not only tough, they also produce the most brilliant pendulous bract flowers. And there doesn't seem to be a set flowering period – they just arrive, most welcomely, when you least expect them. Very easy care.

Bougainvillea
The bract flowers are brilliant beyond words, but these are perhaps not strictly houseplants. Better suited to the conversatory that offers modest warmth in winter and good light in summer. Very easy to care for, they shed their leaves in winter and come into growth and flower about the same time in early spring. For the best possible effect train growth to a wall trellis.

Bougainvillea hybrid 'Miss Manila'

33

Brunfelsia calycina
Flowering over a long period, the common name of Yesterday, Today and Tomorrow refers to the changing colour of the flowers over a three-day period, from violet-purple to almost white. This compact, evergreen plant can be lightly pruned if branches become untidy. Offer good light and temperature in excess of 18°C (65°F) for best results. Moist conditions are essential but give less water during the winter months. Feed well when in active growth; avoid overpotting.

Calathea
Very colourful foliage is the trade mark of these exotic, but somewhat delicate plants. Temperature in excess of 18°C (65°F) is essential; also shaded and moist conditions. Some are only for the experienced plantperson, but *C. lubbersiana* is one that seems more tolerant of room conditions.

Campanula isophylla
Easy to propagate from cuttings and now available from seed, these are fine plants with heart-shaped, mid-green leaves, suitable for small hanging pots. There is a blue and a white form; the latter being the easier to care for. Offer them a bright window location out of strong sunlight, and keep the compost moist but not saturated. If the dead flowers are carefully picked off the plant will go on producing flowers for many months.

Chlorophytum capense
'Variegatum'
The Spider Plant rates as one of the toughest of our foliage houseplants and has been with us ever since indoor plants were first introduced. Easy to manage, it loves to grow in a hanging container with its baby

Campanula isophylla 'Alba'

plantlets suspended on attractive yellow stems. Leaf tips are inclined to brown if potting and/or feeding is not regularly attended to. Light, airy and reasonably warm conditions will suit this plant.

Cineraria 'Starlet' mixed

Cineraria
The sort of annual, colourful pot plant that you may well consider raising from seed if you have a greenhouse with a modest amount of heat. It bears masses of daisy flowers in a good range of colours. Pests are a problem and seem to come in all varieties, so a keen watch should be kept for these with a view to using an appropriate insecticide. Cool and light conditions are best.

Citris mitis

Citrus mitis
Most citrus plants are too large for the average room, but the Calomondin Orange is a compact plant that fruits freely after bearing fragrant white flowers when happy with its lot. Offer good light, moisture and modest temperature for success. Watch for scale insects and red spider mites.

Clivia miniata
A South African native with leathery evergreen leaves that emerge from thick basal stems, and flowers with rich orange colouring. Given good light, reasonable temperature and considerate potting on these make fine specimens in time; 20-30 stems of bloom not being unusual. Keep in reasonable light, warm and moist conditions for good results.

Codiaeum
Better known as crotons or by their common name of Joseph's Coat, there are numerous varieties with brilliantly-coloured foliage, the leaves being either broad or narrow. Temperature in excess of 18°C (65°F) is essential, also good light and compost that is never allowed to dry out. Feeding in spring and summer is also a must. When potting use a John Innes No 3 mix. Red spider mites can be a problem in conditions that are hot and very dry.

Columnea
Lovely plants for hanging containers, there being green and variegated forms. The green form *C.* × *banksii* is one of the easiest to cultivate and one of the most floriferous. In normal conditions flowers appear in January/February and are in lovely orange/yellow shades. Provided plants are kept warm and moist, and in good light, there are few problems. They ought to be much more popular than they are.

Crassula argentea
Originally the Jade Plant, but in recent years more popularly known as the Money Plant, these are succulents that tolerate a lot of misuse without showing signs of distress. Keep them in good light, modest temperature and avoid the temptation to water too frequently; little, if any, is needed in winter. Besides the green form there is a nice variegated one.

Crassula argentea

Cryptanthus

These are among the smallest of the Bromeliads and because of their star shape and their tendency to grow at ground level in their native habitat they have the common name of Earth Stars. Very slow growing and relatively easy to care for, they are perfect for bottle gardens and terrariums, where the brightly-coloured leaves are very effective. Offer reasonable temperature and light and avoid overwatering or overfeeding.

Cyclamen persicum

Cool, light and airy conditions are essential for these lovely flowering plants that come in a wide range of colours, some with pleasingly variegated foliage. Do not stand them in saucers of water as present-day peat composts absorb far too much water with the result that plants easily become waterlogged, then the roots rot and they die. Remove dead leaves and flower stems regularly to discourage the incidence of botrytis and mildew problems.

Cyclamen persicum 'Belle Helene'

Cyperus

Not everyone's favourite, but these aquatics are nice plants with their tall stems, umbrella-like arrangement of leaves and flowers at the top of each stem. Water, water, water is the cry here, so much so that plants should always be standing in a well-filled dish. Propagate from seed or by division. No problems if watering is attended to. C. alternifolius is the most often seen.

Dieffenbachia picta 'Camilla'

Dieffenbachia

The Leopard Lilies have been much improved over the years and many spendidly-coloured forms are now available. The variety D. picta 'Camilla' has foliage that is almost entirely creamy white with the narrowest possible margin of green. Dieffenbachia are sensitive to bacterial diseases, but provide light shade, temperature in excess of 18°C (65°F) and moisture at their roots and they will not be too troublesome.

36

Dizygotheca elegantissima

The plant with the difficult name that is probably better known as *Aralia elegantissima*. The filigree leaves are almost black in colour and are carried on tall, upright stems, but it is not a beginner's plant. Light shade is best and temperature of not less than 15°C (60°F) with careful watering that ensures the compost does not remain sodden for long periods; this is especially important in winter.

Dracaena

Lots of these, from the tiny *D. rededge* to the majestic *D. deremensis* that will attain a height of some 3m (10ft) when growing in a pot in conditions that are to its liking. Good light, but not direct sunlight, and compost that is never too wet are best. The toughest of them all is probably *D. marginata* which has thin green leaves with a dull red margin and a rather graceful arching habit that is most pleasing.

Dracaena deremensis

Dracaena marginata 'Tricolor', both tough and graceful

Episcia dianthiflora

Not the plant of the commercial grower of houseplants, but nice for hanging containers nevertheless, and one that produces interesting white snowflake flowers that give the plant its common name of Snowflake Plant. Everything should be reasonable – the light, the temperature, the watering and the feeding. Small rosettes of leaves can be propagated easily.

Euonymus japonicus

One of the nicest of outdoor evergreen shrubs, the smaller-leaved forms have captured the interest of the houseplant producers and there are now numerous varieties available as 'houseplants'. But they are good value in that they are very easy to care for, and can be planted out of doors to grow on when they begin to lose their sparkle.

Ficus robusta

Our old friend the Rubber Plant has been around for as long as we have known houseplants and is still reasonably popular with the plant-buying public. It sheds leaves if too wet at the roots in winter, but is easy to care for if given agreeable conditions in summer, and no food and little water in winter.

Ficus benjamina

One of the most popular houseplants and one that can grow to a considerable size, the Weeping Fig has evergreen foliage and elegant arching stems that can be either slender or bushy depending on how the plant has been treated. Good light is essential but not bright sun, and the temperature should not fall below 15°C (60°F). Scale insects can be a problem, but the main difficulty for this plant is dark conditions which can result in dramatic leaf drop.

Ficus benjamina (Weeping Fig)

Ficus pumila

Totally different in that the Creeping Fig only gets away from ground level if it can find a wall that is damp and to which its adventitious roots can cling and encourage growth. Moist and shaded conditions are essential, otherwise few problems. Fine plants for terraria and bottle gardens.

Ficus pumila (Creeping Fig)

38

Gardenia jasminoides has fragrant, semi-double flowers of creamy white

Gardenia jasminoides
On the expensive side, but the incredible fragrance of the white flowers will make the purchasing outlay seem quite reasonable. Foliage is evergreen and the semi-double flowers are a lovely creamy white. Offer light shade and reasonable temperature, ensuring that the compost is moist at all times but not allowed to remain sodden for lengthy periods.

Hedera canariensis
One of the many dual purpose large-leaved ivies that will grow either indoors or out. Outside they are perfect as wall plants, or for concealing unsightly objects in the garden. Foliage is white and cream and one of the few problems is the red spider mite. Keep cool, light and never too wet, giving the occasional feed during spring and summer.

Hedera helix 'Gold Child' with its bright golden variegation

Hedera helix 'Gold Child'

Named by Mr Houseplant himself, Thomas Rochford, after his first-born grandchild, this is a very fine plant with bright golden foliage as the name suggests. Buy several small ones and try growing them and nothing else in an attractive hanging pot. You may well find that they are more appealing to you than garishly-coloured flowers.

Helxine soleirolii

A weed if ever there was one, but a weed if properly presented can often outsell its more cultured neighbours and this would certainly seem true of Mind Your Own Business – an amusing common name that is also an encouragement when it comes to selling this creeping plant. Keep wet and in reasonable light (not direct sunlight) and it will be no bother. When overgrown simply clip back and insert a few fresh pieces.

Helxine soleirolii 'Argentea'

Heptapleurum arboricola

Also introduced to Europe by Tom Rochford, this has become one of the most popular of foliage plants; there are also golden coloured forms and all come under the common name of Parasol Plant. They very often shed leaves for no apparent reason, but part of the cause may be excessive temperature. My own plants in a conservatory that is virtually unheated in winter have been doing amazingly well, so cooler conditions could be worth trying if leaf drop is a problem. They can grow to a height of 2.4m (8ft) when happy.

Hibiscus rosa-sinensis

Flowers of these may be single or semi-double, and plants may be deciduous if allowed to dry out in late autumn, or foliage may be retained if soil is kept moist. Bright flowers come in numerous colours and last for but a single day before they shrivel and die. Sad, you may think, but healthy plants will reward your good care by producing a continual succession of flowers throughout the summer so there is ample compensation. Good light is the most important need. Watch out for aphids and red spider mites.

Heptapleurum arboricola 'Variegata' (the Parasol Plant)

Hippeastrum

Another enigma in that you will more often than not find this exotic flowering plant sold as an *Amaryllis*, but they are one and the same. Being a bulbous subject it is perhaps not a true houseplant, although it is much used for indoor decoration. Bought bulbs, or planted bulbs will be little bother on the light windowsill in a warm room, but flowering them for a second time can be difficult. After flowering keep indoors until frosts are over then put out in the garden still in its pot. Feed and water throughout summer, but then withhold water and allow the bulb to rest at the end of summer. Keep warm and dry until January/February, then water and keep as warm as possible to encourage flowering. When into growth place back on windowsill.

Hydrangea macrophylla

Another double value plant that can be planted outdoors after flowering (large heads of pink, blue or white flat florets) inside. Keep very moist when indoors and provide a light and airy location for best results. Be sure to buy sturdy, clean plants.

Hippeastrum hybrid 'Orange Sovereign'

Impatiens 'New Guinea' hybrids have a good range of flower colours

Hypoestes sanguinolenta

At one time a weedy, unimportant plant with wishy-washy silvery foliage, but very different since the bright pink forms were introduced – it has now become one of the most popular of all the smaller foliage plants. Small plants should be potted on soon after purchase and a light location found for them to grow. Pinch out tips to encourage bushy habit. *H. aristata* is the other species of this shrub that is suitable for indoor cultivating.

Impatiens 'New Guinea' hybrids

Some are rather dull, but the bright foliaged forms make fine plants in a light room. Moisture is essential, as is the need for frequent feeding. Water the plant and inspect the roots on purchase with the thought in mind that potting on is a distinct possibility for these greedy plants. Besides nice foliage they offer a good range of flower colours.

Kalanchoe, mixed

Kalanchoe

Lots of these but the most popular by far are the numerous forms of *K. blossfeldiana*, with their succulent fleshy leaves and brightly-coloured flowers. On a light windowsill the flowers seem to go on forever, but potting on of smaller plants will be necessary if full value is to be obtained. Avoid overwatering and feed established plants weekly in spring and summer.

Monstera deliciosa

Monstera deliciosa

The ubiquitous Cheese Plant is still sold in vast numbers. Most are grown from seed, and when purchasing one should seek out specimens that have several young plants in the pot, as opposed to solitary stems. Moist, shaded and warm conditions suit them best. A moss-covered pole as opposed to a bare cane will be more attractive as a support and an encouragement to growth. Eventual height could be up to 3.6m (12ft).

Nephrolepis exaltata

The Boston Fern is an incredibly popular indoor plant that is much featured at all manner of exhibitions, besides in the office and the home. When purchasing, choose plants of full appearance with rich green foliage. Keep them shaded, moist and warm indoors and feed regularly in the growing season. Pot plants on if the foliage begins to lose its lush green look.

Kentia (Howea) forsteriana

The most elegant of all the purely foliage houseplants, these are expensive, but perfect when used as individual specimens. Avoid spraying foliage with leaf cleaning chemicals and watch for paler colouring in foliage which is an indication that red spider mites are active. Light shade is best, and temperature of never less than 15°C (60°F).

Maranta

Several cultivars are available, including *M. leuconeura*, but they are much less popular plants than they were in the past. Keep them warm and avoid bright sunlight to succeed. They are really floor of the jungle plants which prefer shaded locations and a degree of moisture around them. Peaty compost is necessary when potting on.

Nephrolepis exaltata

Primula malacoides (the Fairy Primrose) in a selection of colours

Philodendron

Belonging to the family Araceae, the philodendrons are many and varied, but all are beautiful foliage plants and almost all prefer to grow in shaded, moist conditions in a temperature of not less than 15°C (60°F). The majority have green foliage, but there are the odd few that are variegated (and difficult to grow!) and some with a lovely burgundy sheen. There are few pest problems.

Poinsettia
(Euphorbia pulcherrima)

Flowering naturally just before Christmas, this plant is a real blessing to the grower who is capable of growing it well. Good light is essen-

tial, also a temperature of not less than 18°C (65°F) when in active growth. Indoors, offer good light, warmth and a watering programme that errs on the side of dry rather than wet. White fly can be troublesome if you are not vigilant.

Primula

Numerous species, with *P. obconica* and *P. malacoides* probably having the edge in popularity. Offer cool, light and moist conditions. (Avoid *P. obconica* if you have sensitive skin.) The Fairy Primrose, *P. malacoides*, is the prettiest of plants; several in a selection of colours being a real joy on the windowsill. As a bonus, they are delicately fragrant.

Saintpaulia ionantha (African Violets) are worth cosseting

Saintpaulia ionantha

At some time or other everyone must have tried to grow African Violets – some having dismal failures while others are surprisingly successful. On a north-facing kitchen windowsill, in reasonable warmth, almost everyone should be able to grow them. But to encourage flowering you should offer them additional artificial light in the evening and feed with, say, a tomato fertiliser which is high in potash as opposed to high in nitrogen.

Sansevieria trifasciata 'Laurentii'

Mother-in-Law's Tongue is killed off through becoming too cold and too wet during the winter months – cold and wet at the same time can be death to most plants, particularly those, such as the sansevieria, which have fleshy, succulent leaves. Keep them in good light and otherwise neglect them is my recipe for success.

Sansevieria trifasciata 'Laurentii'

Scindapsus aureus

The white-foliaged *S. aureus* 'Marble Queen' is a difficult plant to care for, but the variety 'Golden Queen', with its bright golden foliage, is very much easier and reasonably reliable in poorish light. Avoid bright sun and maintain a temperature of not less than 15°C (60°F). Can be propagated from stem cuttings.

Spathiphyllum wallisii

Spathiphyllum wallisii

White spathe flowers give this plant the common name of White Sails. Flowers are produced at almost any time during the year, and larger plants will rarely be without flowers or buds that promise flowers. Excellent subjects for poor light conditions if a temperature in excess of 15°C (60°F) can be maintained. New plants are produced simply by dividing up the older clumps at any time.

Stephanotis floribunda

Avoid purchasing these plants during the winter months when they are very much weaker with flowers that quickly go over. Natural climbers, they will need some sort of framework to which growth can attach itself. Keep in a light window location and water with great care in winter. Sudden collapse of plants is usually due to overwatering causing root failure, or the fact that weak winter plants were bought. Their greatest asset is their wonderful fragrance.

Tradescantia

Lots of lovely coloured foliage among these easy-care plants, and all of them reasonably easy for the beginner to manage, and to propagate from stem cuttings placed in water. Hanging pots are the ideal containers, and they should have good light and not be too wet at their roots, particularly in winter.

Tradescantia fluminensis

INDEX AND ACKNOWLEDGEMENTS

Picture credits
Pat Brindley: 17, 28/9, 35 (t), 37(b), 39, 40(t).
Marshall Cavendish Library: 4/5, 6, 16, 44(t).
Harry Smith Horticultural Collection: 1, 7(t), 8, 10, 11(t,b), 12, 21, 22, 25(b), 26(br), 30(t,b), 31(t),
    32(t,bl,br), 33(b), 36(t,b), 37(t), 38(t,b), 40(b), 43(b), 46(b), 47(t).
Michael Warren: 7(b), 9, 18, 19, 24, 25(t), 26(bl), 27(t,b), 31(b), 33(t), 34(t,b), 41, 42, 43(t),
    44(b), 45, 46(t), 47(b).

Artwork by Simon Roulstone